W9-DET-306

Little Stars

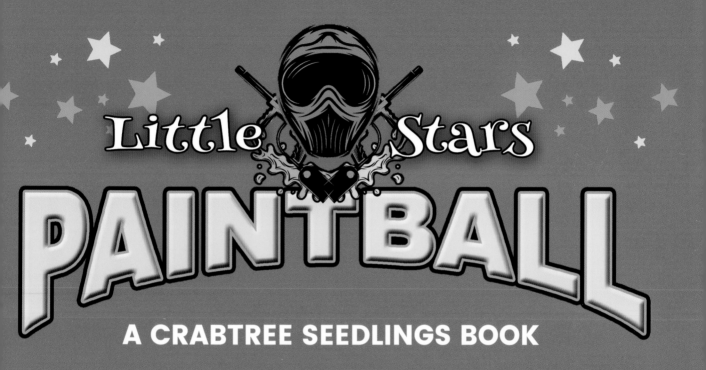

Little Stars

PAINTBALL

A CRABTREE SEEDLINGS BOOK

Taylor Farley

CRABTREE
PUBLISHING COMPANY
WWW.CRABTREEBOOKS.COM

SPLAT!

I just fired my last **paintball**.

3

It marked an **opponent**, so now he is out.

4

I find a place to hide and I reload my **marker**.

My marker has four parts.

barrel

hopper

grip

trigger

9

Paintballs are loaded in the hopper.

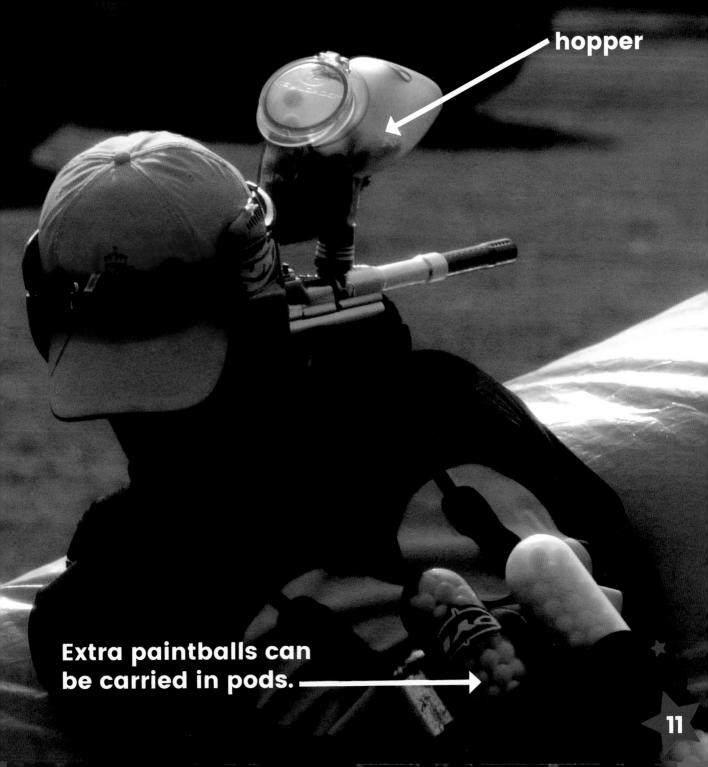

hopper

Extra paintballs can
be carried in pods.

I look around to find **enemy** players.

13

I wear **loose** clothes and a mask for **safety**.

15

I run across the field.

A paintball hits my mask.

18

I am out, but I had fun!

Glossary

enemy (EN-uhm-ee): In paintball, the enemy is any player or team you are playing against.

loose (LOOSS): Loose clothing does not fit tightly and is good for moving around in.

marker (MAR-ker): A marker is a paintball gun.

opponent (uh-POH-nuhnt): An opponent is someone who is playing against you.

paintball (PAYNT-bawl): A paintball is a small, round ball filled with colored paint. Paintball is also the name of the sport where players try to hit opponents with paintballs fired from paintball markers.

safety (SAYF-tee): Safety is being kept from harm.

Index

School-to-Home Support for Caregivers and Teachers

Crabtree Seedlings books help children grow by letting them practice reading. Here are a few guiding questions to help the reader build his or her comprehension skills. Possible answers are included.

Before Reading

- What do I think this book is about? I think this book is about playing paintball. It might tell us about the rules of paintball.

- What do I want to learn about this topic? I want to learn about how paintball players stay safe when they play paintball.

During Reading

- I wonder why... I wonder why paintball players wear loose clothes.

- What have I learned so far? I learned that paintball players wear masks for safety.

After Reading

- What details did I learn about this topic? I learned that there are four parts to a paintball marker: barrel, hopper, trigger, and grip.

- Write down unfamiliar words and ask questions to help understand their meaning. I see the word *opponent* on page 4 and the word *marker* on page 7. The other vocabulary words are listed on pages 22 and 23.

Library and Archives Canada Cataloguing in Publication

Title: Little stars paintball / Taylor Farley.
Other titles: Paintball
Names: Farley, Taylor, author.
Description: Series statement: Little stars | "A Crabtree seedlings book". | Includes index. |
  Previously published in electronic format by Blue Door Education in 2020.
Identifiers: Canadiana 20200379747 | ISBN 9781427129826 (hardcover) | ISBN 9781427130006 (softcover)
Subjects: LCSH: Paintball (Game)—Juvenile literature.
Classification: LCC GV1202.S87 F37 2021 | DDC j796.2—dc23

Library of Congress Cataloging-in-Publication Data

Names: Farley, Taylor, author.
Title: Little stars paintball / Taylor Farley.
Description: New York, NY : Crabtree Publishing Company, [2021] | Series: Little stars: a Crabtree seedlings book | Includes index.
Identifiers: LCCN 2020049296 | ISBN 9781427129826 (hardcover) | ISBN 9781427130006 (paperback)
Subjects: LCSH: Paintball (Game)--Juvenile literature.
Classification: LCC GV1202.S87 F37 2021 | DDC 796.2--dc23
LC record available at https://lccn.loc.gov/2020049296

Crabtree Publishing Company

www.crabtreebooks.com   1–800–387–7650

Written by Taylor Farley

Production coordinator and Prepress technician: Samara Parent

Print coordinator: Katherine Berti

e-book ISBN 978-1-950825-95-0

Print book version produced jointly with Blue Door Education in 2021

Printed in the U.S.A./012021/CG20201102

Photo credits: Cover photo © Iakov Filimonov, cover mask and gun illustration © CHEMADAN, pages 2-3 © Chekyravaa, paint splat © Ramona Kaulitzki, pages 4-5 © Pavel L Photo and Video, pages 6-7 © Chekyravaa, pages 8-9 © Hurst Photo, page 11 © Paulo Oliveira, pages 12-13, 14, 19 © Martin Kovacik, pages 16-17, 21 © Iakov Filimonov
All images from Shutterstock.com

Published in Canada
Crabtree Publishing
616 Welland Ave.
St. Catharines, Ontario
L2M 5V6

Published in the United States
Crabtree Publishing
347 Fifth Ave.
Suite 1402-145
New York, NY 10016

Published in the United Kingdom
Crabtree Publishing
Maritime House
Basin Road North, Hove
BN41 1WR

Published in Australia
Crabtree Publishing
Unit 3 – 5 Currumbin Court
Capalaba
QLD 4157